When There's Only God

*A gang banger's journey from prison to pulpit to **purpose***

JAMES E. FRENCH

PARAMIND PUBLICATIONS
A *Shift* in Thinking

ParaMind Publications

Library of Congress Control Number: 2016916098
ISBN 978-0-9979870-2-7
Printed in the United States of America

Conformity is the jailer of freedom and the enemy of growth.

~John F. Kennedy

Now am I wrong? For trying to reach the things that I can't see?

~Nico & Vinz, Am I Wrong

Dedicated to...

Dillard & Cheryl Davis

Terri L. McCoy
Off Top

Dedications

Than-,kyü\ n.
[fr. A polite expression of appreciation used when expressing one's gratitude.]

I have to take this time to offer my appreciation to so many people, for all their love and support. Family friends individuals and organizations who have contributed to this journey...

Thanks to my mother, father, and grandmother, Mora Lee, Elkon and Effie Mae. Their prayers where never in vain. Thank you Havana for love, respect, support and grand babies, Barbara, Alecia, Vasha, Kayla, Thanks is just not enough for all you have given me. Poise and strategy.

I am blessed to be a "Father" to those four amazing women, and "Granddaddy to six dynamite grand kids...Khadji A. Hunt, Hassan, Aija, Faith, Mariah and DJ.

I am a "God-Dad" (too heck-of-a many to list) and I am "Like a Dad" and Uncle Frenchie to quite a few more.

I wanna take this Moment to say, "thank you" for letting me care about you like I do, you let me coach you, lecture you, laugh with you, and at you.

Thank you for the road trips, parking lots, people watching, Moo Moos & In-n-Out, driving lessons, running out a gas, flat tires, and fishing trips, payday loans, late calls, and the like.

Thank you for the encouragement when my tank is empty, thanks for helping me win. Danika, T.J., Jazz, Ashley D., Hartman, Dom & X, Candis M.

"Thank You" for all the, Dad, Unc, God-dad & Pop moments...I am quite proud to be in your world.

Thanks for being my family.

Vasha thank you for Atari.
Thank you Kimberly Washington.

Chaplain Edward Meads was the Protestant Chaplain of Folsom prison and asked me to lead praise and worship in Folsom prison in 1991 and my life behind the podium began. Chaplain Glenn Shields was Folsom's next chaplain and Pastor Shields is now senior Pastor of Progressive Community Church of Stockton, CA.

Kay & Elvin French (mom and dad). A national prison ministry team known as Joyful News Ministries.

Bob & Penny Lara Tanya & Peterson were like a brother and sister and my first real link with a family in years. Bob, who we call Kentucky Bob, invited me to share the visiting room with he and his family (when I hadn't seen a visitor in eight years) and we are still all close.

Chaplain Ruffin Chaplain at D.V.I. and the visionary behind R.I.C.H. Ministries (Restoring Inmates Community Hope) and P.R.P.P (Parolee Recidivism Prevention Program). These two programs helped changed my life and the lives of many others.

C.J. & Laurie Orndorff and the Second Chance Band. C.J. the band ministered at D.V.I. just months before my parole and told me to look them up in San Diego when I arrived there. I did, and as they say, the rest is history.

Joseph & Mary Roberts gave me a home and family in Fallbrook Ca. Not a place to live, but a HOME. I had never experienced a family bonding like that which the Roberts have allowed me to share with them. Thank you Jordon, Carrie, Jenae, Steve, Teeni, & Jason for your undying love.

Larry & Shellie Bean for sharing their wise counsel about life out here and providing me with a place to hang my hat, and for being there for me even now.

Don A., Grant R., Steiner., L. Gregg, A. Saucier, Ruven S., Chaplain J. Big Eddie, Thomas (Steelers) Freeman, Tonia, and Jamie S., Debra Clark, Orlando G. and all the others, you know who you are, though I could not list all of your names but, I thank you just the same and remind you that your names are listed where it counts, in eternity, with an asterisk for the help you have provided in the crushing of these grapes.

When There's Only God

Table of Content

James E. French

Intro

I am writing this book because I believe in God. My tradition, my training and my testimony all lead to the conclusion that Only God could do what has been done.

Only God could love like this and redeem my life from destruction and crown me with His loving kindness and such tender mercies. Like the never ending views of a diamonds sparkle, there is no doubt that I am seeing God from new angles these days.

There has never been a question if I would write a book. For longer than I care to remember I have been making excuses. Making excuses why I had not shared some of the adventures and lessons of this interesting life of mine. No, it has never been a question would I write something, but rather what would I write about, why would I write it and when would I stop this awful procrastination.

There are so many great works on this topic. Psychologically and Spiritually profound in their investigation of the mandate of God. Sorry, This isn't one of those. This is my expression of 58 years scaling the walls. So, what qualifies me to write a book entitled, Only God? Being an orphan, abandoned at birth, rescued by authorities, placed in foster care, adopted, addicted, convicted and regenerated.

Believe it or not there are a number of qualifiers tucked in the lining of the chaos. It's ironic that seasons and storms that could have washed me away into that sewer of statistics instead planting my feet on a rock and served as my credentials for service.

My qualifications lie in the 58 years I have grouped in the dark on the paths of God. I went to prison dressed in the thug life, but I was indwelled with destiny. The clothes of real manhood were way too big for me then, but they would be waiting.

I tried to teach the qualities that distinguish the man from the boy, while still learning the lessons myself. The world is filled with little boys suffering from so much loss, pain, violence and rage that bullies us. From the schoolyard confrontations to the threats of thermal nuclear war, it can all be traced to the tantrums of an army of little boys. Little boys of every race and creed, with good jobs and fast cars. Little boys with degrees and titles and big money, but little boys nonetheless.

I know this to be truth because it is my story. I became a man, a leader and a teacher while still groping for the paths of manhood and enlightenment.

Why do we need to talk about this? We must talk about it because it has become clear to me that the older I grow, the more it becomes necessary that I take bigger steps in the right direction. I had to take bigger steps towards my purpose. On that journey I reached the end of me. That's when I discovered there was Only God.

James E. French

4

CHAPTER ONE

Origins & Growth

Every happening, great and small, is a parable whereby God speaks to us, and the art of life is to get the message.

> ~Malcolm Muggeridge

Naked Enlightenment

Several shotgun blasts reverberated in the air.

"Down on the yard!" hailed a choir of guards almost in harmony.

One of the guards fired warning shots to quell an altercation between two inmates on the weight pile, same as always.

Before I heard the shots fired, my eye was already on the commotion across the yard, but it was all a routine. The heat outside on the yard was sweltering.

"I don't need this today," I thought.

To make matters worse, here comes the part I couldn't stand the most. Every man had to strip butt naked and lay on the yard as still as a statue, proving he was not concealing a hot shot gun shell in his rectum.

I knew what to do from experience, hell, I had done this for so many years that I never thought twice about it. Now for the first time, I felt humiliated. I didn't feel like a hard core banger handling another state prison routine. This time, I felt like a grown man lying naked on the grass, stripped of his rights paying a debt to society.

Why wasn't I somewhere teaching someone to read? How did I end up here, in this position bound by the weight of my past mistakes?

There was no time for a pity party. The guards footsteps drew closer. Any sudden movement could have result in immediate death as the trigger happy guards watched closely ready to shoot first and justify later. I assumed the position and prepared to follow the drill of *bend over and cough.*

Indignity overwhelmed me like I couldn't believe. There was a consciousness awakening inside of me, a change of sorts that was very unfamiliar. Like one of those many times in my life when the curtain goes down and life gets real.

Why now? From 1977 to 2003, I lived as Convict C-01884. For twenty-three years, plus three years on parole, I served in the old school California Department of Correction which included: Folsom, San Quentin, CMC, Chino, Susanville, Vacaville and Corcoran Security Housing Units.

After all I had done in my lifetime why did I feel like this now? The easiest answer was — time. It was time...God's time. The favor God showed me all of my life, despite my past decisions and actions was finally pushing me in the trajectory of destiny. Something had to change to avoid demolishing the ultimate reward that was intended for me but not recognized.

I couldn't explain my emotions, but I did understand that I had to do more than what I been doing. I had to do more than just waiting for my release date. At thirty years old, I was a rough neck, young thug, with potential. Prison had been a rite of passage, college for the criminal, and I had definitely paid the admission.

My years in prison showed me there is no such thing as happenstance. From the moment of creation to the end of life there was and remains to be a destiny design for each of us. The problem is we often aren't aware of it until we're on our deathbed praying for more time to live or in my case, lying on the grass face down waiting for another man to search your cavity.

On that day the ground did feel like my deathbed and my entire life flashed before me. I couldn't help thinking that this was not what my parents envisioned for my life. Thoughts of my journey and how I got to this point began to consume me.

Growing up French
My earliest childhood memories are of San Diego California and the nice middle-class family that adopted me. There names were Elkon French and Mora Lee French, a couple in their 40s along with Mora's mother, Effie Mae Jones. As a family, they took me in after spending three years in foster care. What a blessing, because when I was born the state of California took me from my biological mother, Patricia. She was alone and hustling in San Diego, which was not the best environment for a new baby, especially after the infant death of her first child.

The name Frederick Lawrence Johnson was given to me at birth. James E. French was born the day I became a new member of the French family.

The French's kept the adoption a secret and raised me as their own. Only my adopted parents and a few others in their circle knew the truth. Despite the sworn secrecy, I found out as the years went on by talking with cousins and hearing conversations. By the time I was fifteen years old, I was convinced that I was from a different bloodline, but had no idea whose line it was. Growing up during the 60s, those kinds of secrets were serious and had the tendency to break families apart. Everybody in the family lied for years to protect my feelings. The lies continued for so long that the lies became the truth. It didn't matter because I was happy. Keeping the secret wasn't a problem as long as I remained with the Frenchs.

Early childhood with the French family was good, except for being an only child. Although I had everything I wanted, I yearned for a companion. Living with two aging parents and my grandmother I often felt lonely.

Despite the solitude, life with my parents was full of exposure, often due to their professions. My mother, Mora Lee was a maid for a number of wealthy families in the San Diego area. The mayor of the city was one of her clients, along with a few Mafioso's who lived in the Carlsbad community where I spent much of my youth. Carlsbad was a rich resort area in Northern San Diego County, California. During my early years, I was right there in the mix partaking in the privileged activities of the affluent.

Every summer, I would either be at camp or a junior lifeguard surfing at Mission Beach. In the winter, I would enjoy snow sports in the Northern California Mountains. It felt good being a kid exposed to the richness of families, neighborhoods and individuals different from myself or people I lived around. My encounters with various people, culture, music, food and entertainment were all things that I would not have experienced if not for my mother's occupation and connections to a world unknown to most black boys. I even developed a life long friendship with Doug T., the son of one of my mother's clients. Doug's dad Mr. T. treated my mom very well.

My mom even had a room at their home for those nights she worked late throwing fancy parties. I have fond memories of her taking me along to spend the night. In between serving guests, mom brought me half emptied trays of hor'sdevours and finger food all night. Those were the best times. I spent so many nights with my mom at their home that I got to know the director's son very well. We were close in age and hit it off instantly. He was like the sibling I never had.

It was nice taking advantage of the perks from my moms job, but she was not only a maid. My mom was also a proud Black business owner. She owned Jewel's Cleaners, a cleaning and pressing shop named after, my Aunt Jewel. My mother was amazing. I often wondered how a woman could stand in front of a steam press day after day in the neighborhood, clean houses, come home and still take great care of me? Mama knew love and I felt it.

My father, Elkon French, also known as Mr. Frenchie in the community, was a Pullman Porter on the Santa Fe Railroad. The Pullman Company was once the largest single employer of African American men in the country. Porters traveled extensively serving travelers and connected their communities to a wider world. At home, they were respected members of their communities. My father was known as Porter 24 and he was lucky enough to be one of the proud members of a rare breed of brothers. He was always sharp in his midnight-blue uniform with gold buttons strategically sewn down the front of his Eisenhower jacket. His signature black cap with the words Pullman Porter embroidered across the front completed the look. I can still hear him shouting out the words, "All Aboard!"

As busy as my parents were, growing up with good Christian values was important in our household. Even though I was raised in a Baptist church, I attended a private Catholic school just around the corner from our home. Mass was held every morning before class at St. Jude and church service was every weekend at Bethel Baptist. I was both an altar boy carrying incense for the priest down the aisle in front of all the students and an usher doing the "Holy Ghost" dance at a revival in the same week. It was awhile before I knew if I was Baptist or Catholic. You can say I was sort of a religious hybrid. I am so thankful for those experiences and other opportunities that stitched the patterns of my life. Looking back, I can say I was provided for and even spoiled in a way not many little black boys in the 1960s from Southeast San Diego could claim. It appeared that the foundation was set for me to have a storybook life, but when I turned thirteen things shifted.

Shifted Trajectory
The public school in my area always had a summer camp for arriving sixth graders, while the Catholic school I attended did not. I wanted to attend the camp very badly but I knew my parents wouldn't approve. So I needed a plan. I've always had the ability of persuading my parents to let me

have my way, and this was no different. That summer, I talked them into moving me over to public school for my sixth grade year. It was a big move for my folks, but I had no idea of the repercussions the move would have on me. That year, my whole world changed.

It was the beginning of integration and several kids from my neighborhood including myself were being bused out to school.

I enrolled at Oak Park Elementary school. The bus route to North County was 45 minutes.

In Catholic school, I didn't have access to many black kids. Attending private school was unheard of for most black families in the 60s, so I didn't see kids from the neighborhood at my school. Riding the bus allowed me to blend in. I quickly gravitated to the black kids at Oak Park in a way that I had not done before. The expectations of my new peers were different. Now I had to fit in. For one thing, I never cursed and the other kids did. Once I tried it, I liked it. My new friends and I formed a tight group and kept each other covered. We had our brother's and sister's back, so to speak. The truth was we had to be ready to defend ourselves when that homebred racism reared its adolescent head and said, "Nigger!"

Many people didn't support integration, which left us exposed to people hurling paint as well as insults at us as we waited for the bus to take us home. Despite the risk, we stood together as one. We were a unified body but I needed to step it up.

My little Catholic school training was kicked to the curb. I soon learned to talk, look and act crazy on cue. If I wanted to survive integration with my crew, this was a requirement.

The learning curve was intense. Who I was trying to be deep inside was not the real me. It took me a minute to get my act right. I had to be an excellent actor for the majority of my life convincing myself and others that I was a brother and I belonged there. I had to show them that their world was my world too.

Perception quickly became reality. For five years I went to school at the big Catholic church with a group of little kids in uniform. I knew all the nuns and priest. They viewed me as one of the smart, privileged kids. Now, I was acting tough, bussed to school with many of the kids my mother hadn't let me play with previously. She said they were dangerous and she wanted to protect me. At the time I had no idea what she was trying to protect me from, but it would not take long to see my mother had cause for concern.

The kids who took the bus used to see me walking from chatholic call me "church boy" when I would walk past their bus in my uniform previously. Now I was getting on the bus cussing trying to be cool. I didn't care how the kids used to see me. The only thing that mattered was that I was going to school with them and proud to finally be one of them. I'll admit I was green, but being with these kids everyday made me a part of their family. If I didn't fit in, I risked being ostracized.

When I started in the public school system it was loud and clear that I was discovering something about myself that I had not known. I yearned for those bad talking, pot smoking, long lost cousins that my mother told me to leave alone. Now that I knew them, they were pretty cool. That's where my shift started.

Exploring this new lifestyle felt like I had known it my whole life, but never had the guts to try it out. It probably felt similar to what a business graduate feels felt like after taking a big leap into the business world and closing a million dollar deal. This had to be what it felt like after writing your first novel and it lands on the best seller's list. I felt like I won, but I was accepted into a world that I was not prepared for.

I discovered that I could fight, I could dance, I could talk shit and I knew how to be quiet when I needed to be quiet. I was adapting to my new world, oblivious to where I was headed. The lure of something new was tugging on me. I would ultimately follow it's seductive pull down a path that had the potential to take me out and nearly did.

When There's Only God

James E. French

18

CHAPTER TWO

Old Game

In the desert, the only God is a well.
~Vera Nazarian

Glitter in the Street
By the time I was in seventh grade at Horace Mann Junior High School I was smoking weed. Not to mention my grades were free falling. In exchange, I was learning my way around and getting comfortable in the company of my new crew.

This wasn't the type of comfort my parents imaged or wanted for me. I knew they could see the shift in my behavior. It was apparent. I started stealing to satisfy my new habits and buying other treats for my friends who thought my family had money. They came to expect me to buy these treats to indulge. I needed to feed my wants which mainly consisted of at least a nickel sack of weed.

My boys and I looked forward to that high daily, but I always needed a little more.

I was worrying my folks to death and then the arrests started. Early on it was for truancy, but soon evolved into real criminal activity. It was all intentional and part of my plan. I needed to prove I was 'down.' I could not keep getting good grades, having teachers like me and receiving awards. If I was going to fit into the dysfunction that was becoming my world, I had to earn my respect. In rebellion, every now and then I cursed out a teacher. After class, I would secretly talk to the teacher to apologize and make up for my behavior. Maybe I was attempting to tow the line and hold on to my true self which was rapidly fading and eventually disappeared.

Many of the adults around me knew I had potential, but it was being misdirected and they didn't understand why. To me it was clear. I had to assimilate to be accepted, or so I thought. A fallacy I structured much of my young life around. It led me to a dark place I had never envisioned.

I had to earn my credibility by showing I didn't care about much. The reality was I did care and I was often scared, but I could never let it show. Caring and fear were all signs of weakness that gave off a stench which permeated through the air to be sniffed out by the wolves whom I called my crew.

As my popularity grew, my life continued to spiral. I was making an investment in my future, throwing rocks at the penitentiary but it wasn't the future I had been told was possible. I was investing in a life that led to a dead end. My vision was too clouded to see where I was headed. Blinded by the unity and the respect I received, my behavior became worst. I was a young man with a few skills and abilities that should have been nurtured early rather than being fed by the streets becoming poisoned by the environment I frequented.

One of the big differences in the kids within my circle, versus the kids up North, they had resources. Their parents invested money into them to nurture their skills. They identified the talents their children possessed and connected them to resources to foster those talents. In contrast, the kids in my circle had to identify those talents on their own. They hoped to find a teacher or mentor that cared enough to foster those talents.

I was without the knowledge of what I was capable of. I was willing to abandon my gift for something much less valuable or rewarding. This was and would continue to be the plight of many

21

living with similar circumstances. It was the little kid that didn't know he could play the saxophone because he didn't have the exposure, the resources or the person to guide him and bring insight to who he was and what he possessed. It was the little girl who could naturally sing like an angel, but didn't have anyone to help her develop her gift to share with the world. When you don't become acquainted with it early enough it is often, tragically traded, for the glitter in the streets.

The Streets
I was taught the gospel early in life. I learned that Jesus died for my sins, a condition I gained at birth and maintained by virtue of my sinful tendencies. I heard of repentance, atonement and adoption. I heard faith, grace and mercy. I memorized scripture, but that was just my tradition, my subculture so to speak. I was learning the value of staying inside of my Christian subcultural boundaries. It was more monkey-see-monkey-do, than learning the real value of the "Messiah's Message." A message of unity not division, coming together not crossing our arms and drawing lines in the sand. A message about putting others first.

I had been taught that faith comes by hearing and hearing by the word of God. Through such teaching, it's easy to put too much value on just being present while the word is spoken, but just listening and not knowing what it is you're listening to is worthless.

Confused by the rhetoric of a misguided subculture I was destroying the dream my family had for that little boy they adopted. My parents tried to stop my spiral to curb the hurt, but it didn't work. I can only imagine the harbored feelings of helplessness that became a constant companion to them. I was being influenced by the voices of individuals who had already succumbed to the streets. My parents saw it happening, but they were old and constantly manipulated by me. I played the part of the innocent kid although in my mind I was a man. When you are constantly experiencing the evils of society or the lower state of human behavior, you begin to believe that's all there is. I began to understand that there was not a bit of difference between the people in my circle and people who worked on Wall Street.

Most people can't understand how people live like I did, but once you start "Set Tripping" you believe that that's the end of it. The environment we dwelled in had shown us that there were two ways out, death or prison and both were on my heels.

By the time I was seventeen I had dropped out of school and was running with thirty year old criminals who had already served time, but were still as stupid as they were at seventeen. They were making money rapidly and they had the neighborhood fearing them, but lived in constant fear themselves. They were the infamous figures most would avoid because they knew their presence meant trouble, but they were my family. Their names spoke volumes as the tales of their criminal activity spread through Southern California like urban legend. These tales gave them an iconic status which to many would seem insane, but to us it meant respect.

From bad to worst
By 1976 I was an addict with a record, my girlfriend was pregnant and we were getting married. I was a Father before I was a husband, and a husband before I became a man. I had no idea how to fill either role. I was kicked out of multiple high schools, I barely went and now I was going to be a father.

My government name was James French, but on the streets I was *Casper*. Casper was my gang name, which meant I was dead "but still here" and well respected in the streets. The police were always on my trail and my parents were hating what I had become. Their little Catholic school scholar was now a full fledge fool and had abandoned all which they worked hard to place inside of me.

When you're around people that always had stacks of money and threw around thousands, you catch the run-off just because you're in proximity to them. I would make drop offs and pick ups for the OGs as needed. I was the little orphan kid who was always down, therefore kept a few bucks in his pocket.

By the time I was nineteen my father was a full fledge alcoholic while my mother spent a large amount of her time in church, probably praying for her wayward son. My parents were mixing like oil and water. I couldn't help to think that I had driven them both to their respective locations. Their delinquent drug using, gang banging son was adding extra stress as they never knew when the call would come, the call that I had been arrested or worse — killed.

My grandmother also lived with us and was a very strong inspiration in my life because of her godly character, but my will to roam free was overwhelming so not even her bible verses or quickness with a switch could deter me.

I think about the nostalgia of my grandmother sitting on the porch snapping green beans and realize that life for me had been that simple as it was for many before we decided to abandon it.

My first marriage was to my first girlfriend Jeannie. I was too street to honor what I had in Miss Walker. I disrespected her and our house, I always had people in and out. Dope and guns were constant fixtures. I was a mess and the situation was worst!

My days were spent plotting robberies which had become my main source of income. It wasn't long before the police started closing in on me. I was able to elude them for months, by staying on the move. I was hiding out all over L.A. I was in contact with my parents from time to time, but couldn't tell them anything. I couldn't tell them what was really going on. During this time they were watching my daughter Shalonda because they knew I wasn't equipped to keep her. I would try to call to speak with my baby or stop by to see her, but they rarely allowed it because they knew the trouble that followed me.

I can remember the time they allowed me to pick her up to spend some quality time with her. I must have sounded pitiful. I think they felt bad for me so they gave me a chance. I picked up my daughter and niece who was there as well and after a short ride around the neighborhood the police spotted me and began to give chase. I punched it! Now on a high speed chase trying my best to elude the cops with two little girls in tow.

There were several times I thought they would catch me, but I was able to get away across a narrow bridge and got them back to the house. They were both laughing, thrilled that I had given them such a cool ride. They never new we were being chased and just recently were reminded of the story.

I pulled up to my parents house and said, "Don't say anything to Grandma and Grandpa."

The next time I saw my daughter was one of the wake up calls that I paid attention to. I was on Parole at our house, Shalonda was about 8 years old and was playing in the front yard while I was in the house. A police car rolled down our street. Once she saw it, she ran into the house, grab my hand and pulled me into a bedroom at the back of the house. She closed the door and stood in front of me, shivering, because she didn't want the police to take me. I was beginning to see how my actions were effecting those around me who cared about me, but it didn't stop me.

The police eventually caught me on a taxi cab robbery. I remember them pulling me over and walking to the car to pull my T-shirt up to see if I had the tattoo they were looking for. After coming back to the car they lifted my shirt again to confirm what they saw and of course they had found it, a ghost along with the name Casper.

I've often hear people say, "Why didn't he just stop, he knew he was going to get caught eventually."

What many people don't understand is that that was my life. This is what I did and I justified it as my existence. One of the many occasions when I was paroled from jail after a short stay. I got out on parole and the police dropped me off at the bus station. When they dropped me off I robbed the gift shop located inside of the bus station. That was my thought process, it was learned behavior.

Each time I was arrested I was given probation. I never did any juvenile time. I was one of those rare adults in the Department of Correction that didn't have a juvenile record. My arrest were dropped or I was given a deal with probation, until that taxi cab robbery. That earned me the "joint suspended" sentence for the time that had accrued. This meant they took the time they had been holding for me (probation has a catch) off the shelf and gave it to me as well. I received 15 years of enhancement to an eight year robbery conviction for the cab, which gave me a 23 year sentence.

I couldn't blame anyone but myself. I thought I was the man with a plan, but what I had was a bizarre hunger for attention that was growing. It caused me to do crazy things to keep my reputation. I was just a two-bit thief with a cheap dope habit and low budget game.

I was trying to talk big talk to impress violent friends. I was living a life of street dreams, which was more of a literal nightmare. Now I was headed to San Quentin prison and it was the streets that took me there.

James E. French

CHAPTER THREE

Original Game

Only God can turn a mess into a message.

C-01884
The first time I walked inside the state Penitentiary in Chino Calif, I was a young, tender faced, pretty boy with long hair. People warned me of how dangerous that could be, but when you got a little gangsta about yourself, you feel like you can handle any situation.

Somehow, I always knew that it was just a matter of time before I would get a pass to prison. I was facing real life and had to adjust rapidly. It was slowly setting in my mind that this was going to be my home for the next 23 years.

Inside I spent a lot of time doing many things to occupy my time, like watching TV, playing chess and hanging out on the yard. I was connecting to the Los Angeles Bloods who would lay the template I began to follow. When they started talking crazy, I started talking crazy, similar to my time on the bus in middle school. I knew when to shut up and how to stay down for my people. I didn't like who they didn't like. That's what doing time was like in a nutshell.

Adapt and follow

Being on the inside soon resembled life on the corner. The biggest difference was that you couldn't go anywhere you wanted and you were told what to do. You just kicked it with all your folks, talked trash everyday and stayed ready to scrap. I develop a daily routine and it became my program as I was living for soups, cigarettes, a phone call and a visit.

I quickly learned that the visiting room itself was considered to be sacred ground. You see there was always a truce in the visiting room no matter what was going on. You could help your enemy find room to sit with his family, help his son tie his shoes, but shank that fool when you got back to general population and that's just the way it went down. I always saw the visiting room as an amazing place the few times I was there, as visitors were uncommon for me. I felt like the visitor's room was a true indication of what was really going on inside the minds of all the men who had enough sense to make the priority the priority at the right time.

I served 23 years and I never saw and rarely heard of that sacred place being violated. Everyone knew if a melee broke out the kids were going to get hurt and no one wanted that. On the yard it was business as usual. We all had one-track-minds and survival was the order of each day.

If that kind of visiting room common sense was displayed by inmates in more areas, prison reform would be an easier sell. Instead prison inmates and the institution itself remain stuck in time and operate with a religious loyalty to the their own detriment. Gang violence and prison politics continue year after year. Little progress is made to move social opinion about crime and punishment. Little progress is ever made to unite behind the truth that we are all in this together.

Old habits die hard

Over the years, I moved around to different prisons. Mainly because the prison officials didn't want the prisoners to become a mainstay or power broker of sorts. From Folsom to San Quentin to Deul Vocational Institution, to Corcoran SHU, I have served time in them all and understood the politics that followed me to each.

I wanted more from life, wanted to do more, but now I was locked down and it was difficult to see past the cell that had become my home. It felt like I was stuck in a bad dream that would not end or a perpetual state of hell, paying for my sins. I was searching for peace surrounded by a sea of evil, negativity and anger.

There was a shift occurring, but my vision was still clouded. My unruly behavior in "general population" sent me to the SHU (Secure Housing Unit), in Folsom. While on the mainline or general population, a few of the homies and I put together a heist of the prison canteen. We plotted and planned just like we did on the outside. We made fake ID's and passed them out to a couple of the homies, The goal was to steal other inmates' money because we had someone on the inside that worked in the canteen and gave us access to all of the inmates accounts to help us.

With fake ID's in hand, all we had to do is walk up to the canteen window and gain access to their accounts and steal the funds until we got caught. I was immediately placed in an indeterminate SHU program which meant I could possibly do the rest of my time in the SHU.

The SHU was like a prison inside of the prison. You are confined to a small cell for 23 hours a day. I was allowed to come out for 30 minutes to shower and 30 minutes for exercise, which consisted of me being able to stretch and pace the floor in a tiny cage the size of a phone booth.

That is where I met Danny C. Danny was a "Double OG." He could have been the uncle Kevin Hart talks about in his stand up Seriously Funny who served fifteen years in the pen, "Uncle Richie Jr."

"Say it with ya' chest!"

He was a straight convict with a mind and heart that was searching for truth, but Danny was still a gangster. I could relate to him because he was just like me. I determined that we were and remain to be very much like the Disciples from the Bible.

Those men were quite "unbecoming" and rough. Think about it, Peter spent three years studying under Jesus. He had the keys to the kingdom, walked on water for a quick minute and saw the transfiguration. But Peter would also still stick a knife in you, curse you out, and lie when he was scared.

Danny was a teacher that became a guide in my life. He opened my mind and heart to God again. It didn't take me long to accept that there was more than this maze I was in.

My flight from the knowledge would have to end here. What he was saying was familiar. It was wisdom I had turned my back on previously in exchange for a word from gangsters that had no feelings. What I was hearing from Danny was a message laced with the importance of surrendering and seeing the bigger picture.

I had to ask myself, "What is the violence and the anger and dishonesty really doing what is it accomplishing?"

Danny explained, "You are meant to set the tone, but instead, you're just playing the same melody of the other men in here who see themselves as victims to the streets."

His words resonated in my spirit. He was the catalyst for me to shift my thoughts and perspective. I began thinking and reading more causing me to consider things differently. Until then, I was confined to the lifestyle of my peers dancing to someone else's music, accepting all I heard as truth, challenging nothing. Now the skies were opening and I was learning some valuable lessons.

Reading's Rainbow

Through my years of school I was required to read, but that's where it stopped. I only read what I had to read in school so I can't say I read to comprehend. I just read to get by. I didn't read to enjoy the text. I never thought about reading to learn or grow, but since I was in the hole I had time to read. It felt like the first time I had read a book. Once I started, I fell in love with the written word and internalized everything I read.

One extremely influential book was, "Manchild in the Promised Land" by Claude Brown. This book painted vivid pictures of the journey of a young brotha through the treacherous streets of Harlem during the 1940s and the 50s.

Brown shared his own story of survival against all odds. Reading that novel about Brown's life felt like an authentic account of the evolution from tough, hardened street fighter. That was familiar to me.

I could relate in so many ways to a young man on the brink of becoming a powerful contributor to the urban African American experience. Brown's novel gave me hope that my life may still have purpose. It inspired me because I could now see possibility in my own story, but also learned that I could be touched by

37

words. I was able to scale the pervedbial wall that often kept me confined within my own mind of limited possibilities. Once I began reading I was sure to always learn something valuable. I was laying up in the penitentiary, on my bunk with a book on my chest, but in my mind I was walking down the streets seeing everything the author spoke of.

Captured by how the author's words become a movie in my mind. I could hear the sounds of the neighborhood, feel the wind on my neck, smell the smoke from the grill and experience the vivid colors he described. It felt like I had a front seat at a feature film.

"Manchild in the Promised Land" led me to "Invisible Man" by Ralph Ellison, another relevant, award winning story of a black man's experience in America.

Another book that helped establish my new world of reading was called, "The Talisman." It's about a little boy who went on an adventure because of a piece of jewelry he had around his neck. What a trip that was.

Reading made me feel like I had been blind my entire like, and now I was able to see for the first time. My eyes were opened to a world that many had already seen and experienced, but it was new to me. It was a world full of hope, dreams and purpose.

I was able to go over the wall in a book. It didn't matter if it was a novel, poetry, social science, advertising or marketing. I was turning on books like you turn on the TV. There were books all over the place, but not on shelves. In prison you didn't get to go and select the book of your choice, so when you started enjoying to read you find any book that's laying around.

Books allowed me to start my escape from the gang life. I was yet to discover who I really was, but what I was learning is that as long as I still had breath in my body, this journey was not done. I read everything I could get my hands on and began looking for more information about life anywhere I could find it. My search ultimately led me back to the Bible. I came upon a study about humility. This was my first real study and it resonated with me immediately. I began taking notes and was desperate to climb over the walls of ignorance that confined me to this hell.

It starts with humility

Humility is defined as a quality by which a person considering his own defects has a humble opinion of himself and willingly submits himself to God and to others for God's sake. It's a virtue.

We often miss this value because humility starts your recognition of your place in this whole thing.

My lesson in humility taught me that I'm not all that. Even when I'm standing on top of the mountain, I'm not all that. I wasn't just created, I was created for a purpose, therefore in my mind there was not a question of the Creator's existence.

The question I began to ask myself was, "Who created the creator?"

A theological perspective I learned about was called the "Ontological View" is one of the arguments for the existence of God. It began with realizing that I was not the biggest thing out here. This can be enhanced by understanding the concepts of deity. Everything begins through something that had to exist before it, so therefore something must exist to itself or be the true original that depends on nothing. We call this something God.

When I consider the Cosmos not having a roof out there, that means there's a forever and ever that exist. Think about it, if you could split an atom repeatedly and each time you split it you had two more whole atoms. This reinforced the idea of my smallness in the universe. It all started to make more sense to me. It was something I needed to know and

I could no longer avoid it. This awakening was the beginning of something big that would push me to the next level of understanding even though I wasn't able to see it in it's totality.

I was gaining clarity, my focus was developing and I owed my new sight to Danny. He had an influence on me that made me thirst for more knowledge. I was getting something from this stuff, but I still had that OG attitude, similar to Peter. I was gaining wisdom and I would never be the same again.

CHAPTER FOUR

Operation Grace

Don't judge someone because they sin differently than you.

Adapt and follow
Prison squeezed me like a toothpaste tube with only a drop left inside. It took me over ten years to feel that way, but now I did.

During those ten years I became as coldhearted and dangerous as I had faked beforehand. Prison was violent and survival of the foolish was the reality. I fought and would have died for things that those on the outside may have seen as trivial. Conformed to the politics of prison, I rode the roller-coaster of incarceration. Prison was now my theme park minus the fun.

My testimony is not the fact that I served time in prison and had to adapt to prison life, but rather my conversion which happened while I was inside.

My story doesn't even begin until I found and became reconnected to the faith that was instilled inside of me long ago.

Yes, my parents and grandmother spoke of faith often, but it was their faith that they spoke of when I was a boy. I was yet to experience that type of faith. Now that prison enslaved man would soon find it for himself.

The incredible way in which God used me and blessed me with a story that became my ministry is the real testimony of my life that cannot be denied.

My first ten years in prison was broken up by brief parole periods where I sat and ticked like a time bomb that reentered society waiting for the violation clock to explode. On my last sentence in 1986, I was given twenty-three years for armed robbery and prior convictions, of which I served thirteen years straight.

Five years into that sentence in 1991 while isolated in the SHU for robbing the canteen in Folsom, I saw a motivational speaker by the name of Les Brown on television. Les said a number of interesting things that really grabbed my attention. There was one thing in particular he said that I just could not get off my mind. Les looked right at the camera and pointed his finger directly at me and said, "Your best days are still ahead of you!"

It was branded in my brain as if those words were spoken just for me. As I look back over my journey I can honestly say that remains to be a true statement, but it was difficult to see it at the time. I believe it is true for you, as well, Your best and brightest days are ahead of you!

This fact became more evident to me on my thirty-third birthday as I sat in a cell preparing to do what we always did. My cellmate had gotten a little weed and we had a little jailhouse wine called Pruno. We were in our cell ready to get high. At that very moment a strong feeling overcame me. It was similar to what I felt while lying on the yard, but this time I could not control my emotions. I found myself just sitting there all emotional about God, life, death and all of my bad choices. I didn't even want to smoke.

I have always spoken about that night in my cell in real religious terms, but all I know is my life changed in that moment. That night on my thirty-third birthday in a cell in Folsom I decided once and for all that I was going to be a new man.

The Power of the Master Number 33 gave new meaning to my life. There are so many analogies of why I felt the power of 33. It was Jesus' age at death and the number 33 is connected to the promises of God. In the book of Genesis, Noah's name is used in scripture 33 times before God makes the eternal promise to not destroy the entire world again with a flood, sealing His pledge with the sign of the rainbow. Abraham's name is used in the bible 33 times before Isaac, the child of promise was born to him when he was 99 years old.

I did not know all of this at the time but felt the weight of the moment as I learned that there are also many examples of the power of 33 that exist beyond the Bible. My studies soon led me to more truth about the master number 33 and it's life path that vibrates through my journey. My truth had been gang banging, representing my set and knocking out cats who disrespected me or anyone in my circle.

I knew that I was changing, maybe subconsciously these facts were influencing me. It was and remains easy to be seduced by this culture. As a 33 year old convict, I had to do something different.

It was not long before I turned into the guy that was always helping, always giving. I was mainly trying to give hope to the hopeless.

Favor is in the trajectory of destiny. I had a favor on my life that was allowing me an opportunity to walk in the gift I was given. The men that surrounded me in prison were missing the ultimate reward that was intended for them. By not recognizing or being scared to embrace their trajectory they stayed shackled in ignorance unable to progress.

Overcoming Odds
Education has always been the key to progression that many prisoners lacked, but with the government shutting down programs prisoners remained stifled. The Violent Crime Control and Law Enforcement Act barred individuals incarcerated in the U.S. from receiving Pell Grants. This new law effectively ended higher education in prisons across the country. Approximately 350 programs around the nation shut down for lack of funds, so reform was becoming an anomaly for many in prison.

A college program at San Quentin was founded in the wake of this travesty and initiated by a professor from UC Davis with Patten College along with members of the Education Department at San Quentin. The program began in the fall of 1996 with two classes, a volunteer coordinator, and no budget.

A preacher from Oakland, California was walking the yard one day registering men in Patton College. He told me they were giving out degrees to inmates who went through the program. I signed up and in three years I graduated.

Eighty people started, but only four people graduated. That was the first time I completed something since I was a kid.

I started frequenting the chapel, meeting the brothers and becoming a regular participant in their studies and services. The Christian faith was a familiar foundation making it easier to embrace messages of love, humility, transformation and redemption.

I don't think I ever really ran from the message more than I ran from religion, organizational extras, judgement and control that dominate this Western presentation of the Messiah's message.

Professor Ron Burris was my instructor, now the senior pastor of Temple Baptist Church in Richmond, California. He was the first person to challenge me to read and analyze God's word. The power of God's message ministered to my heart and changed my mind. I started to live like I believed it.

Before taking the word to heart, I read it relentlessly and even memorized a few choice verses, but I never really examined it. I certainly never lived out the principle inside His word.

I could not intimidate Rev. Burris with my worldly speculations about life and politics. He knew the Word and shared it with skill and a love that was hard to refuse. His character was known and rooted in God. He won my respect, so I studied. I learned theology, books of the Old and New Testament, miracles, evangelism and the list goes on.

The brothers in the prison started coming to me with their problems. Many of my homeboys were also going to church since my conversion experience.

Looking back I knew that I had to do more with my life than what I had been doing. I was given a faith filled foundation, but I did not believe the Bible. The word wasn't real because it was not demonstrated. I abandoned it because of the messenger.

I have been as many would say, "upheld," because of my solid faith filled foundation. I did not just get it in the pen, It was always inside of me, but I didn't believe it. Now it was obvious to me that there was no way I would have survived anything I put myself in the middle of and still be here to write this book. I have no doubt that it was destined, but I had to be able to see over the wall that often blocked my view.

Over the wall

I was told for so long that there was nothing over the wall of benefit. When I say the wall, I speak of that reservoir of knowledge through history, science and philosophy that produce ideas easily avoided in the name of religion. It was my discovery of sound theory that contradicted the black and white worldview of Roman influence. Over the wall there are author's, scholar's, historian's and philosopher's who have devoted their lives to uncover and study the truths in the rocks, the stars and the scriptures. Over the wall there are holy books that weren't holy enough for the councils.

I knew about God from an early age, but I didn't have a real relationship with Him. Raised as a believer and trained in the church. I was called "Lil Preacher" growing up in the church. I have always known in my very being that God is real, alive and active. I just didn't understand what that meant at the time. It was not demonstrated in a way that fostered understanding. I was taught religion over relationship which made me more of a robot rather than a revolutionary.

It wasn't until I began reading that I was driven to revisit the Bible. I was able to see glimpses over the wall. The journey began in the book of Genesis the sixth chapter, but I can't tell you where it will end.

I looked over the wall and I have discovered some interesting things. You've seen the movie where the end of the world is portrayed, and the land over the wall is considered to be the bad land that you are not allowed to venture into, mainly because you were told it was *unsafe*.

When you finally venture out there you find a Coke machine and the only running water. That is what discovering, the study of God, the history of God and the development of God in the minds of men over centuries was like.

The wall is an analogy that helped me understand that there was more, more possibilities to practice faith from a practical perspective. I had to believe that there was something out there for me to discover no matter what others said or what I had previously learned.

I started identifying with my trajectory. I realized that my journey was much more than being a convict, a gang banger or a common run of the mill believer. I would later see that my journey included even more than being a respected local pastor with a portion of truth – now it's time for the whole truth and nothing but the truth.

James E. French

CHAPTER FIVE

Obvious Gifts

What you are is God's gift to you, what you become is your gift to God.

~Hans Urs von Balthasar

A way with words

When I was younger, I could make a person think I had something to say just with my tone, word choice and delivery even if there was no substance. When I started to get wise I began to sound like something worth hearing. When I decided to read things of value, talk about people like they were humans and check myself when I was wrong, my whole world began to expand within the confines of the walls.

After completing my study of humility I read several more books before embarking on a study of self-confrontation. A subject I would teach years later. Self-confrontation says, I will check you on a football score if I think you are wrong. I will even go to the almanac and prove you wrong. When I'm wrong, I do not even want to analyze the situation any longer. I do not want to confront myself. I do not want to take myself to the almanac to prove myself wrong. Whenever things go wrong in my life, even when it is not my fault, I can somehow find the element of truth to gain something from the tragedy or that occurrence. If I can just find the part that I played then I have identified value in that experience instead of being the one that was right. This made me look at myself more and allowed me to reinvent myself. Self-confrontation says I might be wrong even when I sound and believe I'm right, let me almanac my own self to be sure. If I'm not right I keep the lesson and let go of the fallacy.

When I was at DVI (Deuel Vocational Institution) a state prison located in San Joaquin County I had established myself and displayed my value. I was a trusted resource and it showed. I had a key to my prison cell. The lieutenant used to call me out to pray for his family before he got off from work. I was awaken by staff and taken into the gymnasium to calm the feuds between northern and southern California Mexicans. The fact that they had a history of hatred, but were held in the same gymnasium with a fence between them while they were at war clearly demonstrates the authorities manipulation. Both sides would threaten to break down the fence that separated them. I walked down the fence line trying to mediate. Often to little avail but they always let me out alive.

My influence among some of the most notorious criminals in California's history had become one of integrity and commitment. Everybody knew "Frenchie" the chapel clerk.

Prison politics

When you make the decision to not involve yourself in prison politics, you make a drastic choice. For example, if you become a member of the church inside the prison your actions say to the inmate population that you are turning your back on everything they stood for. That is a very difficult decision to make because there ain't no turning back. You live right there in the same little environment with those same people.

Inmates often used the church to hide out from the trouble they have created for themselves or fallen into. That was a reality inside. The brothers who got that respect were some interesting gentleman. They gained it in any type of environment by earning It. They did this by being true to what they believed and folks recognized it. Many still use religion in prison today to hide out as they attempt to outrun their problems, but the problems always seemed to catch up.

Emerald City

When asked how I felt when the time came for me to be released, I have always used the word, *bittersweet*. It may sound strange, but it was evident that prison is where I was needed and I thought I needed prison. I felt that way because it was all I knew.

I assumed the Emerald City similar to the fictional land portrayed in the Frank Braum Oz books was out there, but I had never been there nor did I know how to function out there. For me to come out of prison and start a business or work at a car wash was not very appealing at the time.

I had no choice. I was going to be paroled, but I was still thinking, "What in the world am I going to do on the outside?"

When you are released from prison you must have a job or at least people who are in that community who are prepared to assist you. If you do not have support you find yourself sitting in prison past your date. There are also halfway houses, some of which are places that take you just because you can pay, so people do not have to put in that much work.

I found out where I was going to be placed, about two weeks before I was released courtesy of Elvin and Kay who's last name ironically were

French. This husband & wife ministry team always visited prisons across the U.S.

Whenever they visited our prison I worked in the chapel and always waited for them to arrive. We became family. Kay would perform her Minnie Pearl comedy routine while Elvin sang and preached the gospel.

When it came time for me to parole they were the ones who trusted what they saw in me. Elvin and Kay were so generous, they even bought me a car and paid my rent at a halfway house in Fallbrook California for two years. They are both still in my life today and I will always be there for them. I am a regular guest speaker for Elvin and Kay who I affectionately call dad and mom. They were a major part of my rebirth into the world.

I remain in awe of the opportunity and the way God used them to move in my life. I can't help but to be reminded of how great that is.

Manhood

For a while Folsom had no chaplain. Consequently, we could not have chapel services anymore because we did not have official leadership. Instead we would gather in the bleachers of the gym and baptize each other in laundry carts on Saturday with permission from the staff. Sometimes we had permission to set up in classrooms and have service.

One day the officer working in the kitchen pulled me to the side to tell me that he was thinking about becoming the chaplain. We all knew that Officer Shields was a good cop and a good man. We had not seen him in the role of chaplain so we were eager for him to begin.

I became Shields' chaplain clerk. For several years we saw each other everyday and I knew Shields saw something in me. He recognized how I handled myself, the population and the respect that I earned on the yard by being authentic. The things he saw in me influenced his decision to ask me to assist him on the outside at his church after my release. Pastor Shields was an intricate part of my journey. He also knew I could be trusted and that I was a man of my word.

God was making a way that I definitely had not seen. Although I had faith that He would do it, I just did not know how. I really believed in His word and I knew that God was directing my journey. Now it was becoming evident and I was prepared to venture into the Emerald City with my Bible in tow.

James E. French

CHAPTER SIX

Ordained Glory

People see God every day, they just don't recognize him.
                                                    ~Pearl Bailey

From prison to the pulpit
Sunday morning July 9, 2000, I was released from prison. Pastor Shield sent someone to pick me up in a shiny new Pontiac Firebird Trans Am. It was my first time riding in a car or on a road for that matter in over 13 long years. The car resembled a spaceship inside and it was time for liftoff. We took the 205 Freeway and Interstate 5 to the church. The scenic landscape from Tracy to Stockton was beautiful.

I was headed to deliver my first message and it felt like I was traveling through the stars. It was a scene from the television which had been my only glimpse of real life for years. Here I was finally unchained and unshackled, but still restricted to the conditions of my parole. I was experiencing a liberty that would ultimately free me completely.

When we arrived at Progressive Missionary Baptist Church I went upstairs and I put on a shirt and tie that the First Lady of the church bought for me. She had a brotha sharp as a tack.

The deacons came in the office and I greeted Pastor after not seeing him for a couple years. It was a divine reunion to say the least. We surrounded the Pastor's desk to pray as I learned they did every Sunday.

When it was time for me to speak Pastor addressed me as Reverend French. Everybody shook my hand before I sat down in the pulpit with Pastor Shields like I had done many times before in prison. As I sat in the front of that sanctuary looking at all the people, I could not avoid thinking of how proud my mother would have been to see me sitting in the pulpit about to speak to the congregation. Mom passed while I was in prison, but I knew she saw me standing in this position even when she saw me behind bars. I wish I could have bought her a new hat and gave her a seat in the front row to hear her baby boy's message.

Pastor introduced me with a glowing report about his brother who had been in prison for 20 plus years.

He continued by saying, "I have never met anyone like him. This brother reads Shakespeare. He can give you scientific quotients and most importantly he loves Jesus. This man is a preacher's preacher, so without further ado, I introduce to you Reverend James French."

Two hours out of prison and there I stood in front of a congregation of beautifully dressed people with their eyes fixed on me, to deliver my testimony as I had done for more than ten years while incarcerated. The difference this time was that they didn't look like prisoners, but I knew there was not much difference.

That Sunday Pastor Shield placed his stamp on me and instantly I was *made*. I had become an intricate part of the church. I was Reverend French the *preacher's preacher*.

After service a lovely woman walked up, shook my hand and said, "Your testimony is amazing!"

I replied, "God bless you."

Two years later that woman would become my wife. She was the director of medical ministry and held a master's degree in nursing and hospital administrator. She was a play-write and drama director with three beautiful and brilliant daughters.

The day after our wedding we were on an Alaskan cruise, and the day after returning from our honeymoon I begin traveling, speaking and following Pastor Shields everywhere, carrying his books.

Power in the pulpit

It all seemed surreal. I had been incarcerated for over 20 years, served as the chapel clerk at both Folsom Prison and Deuel Vocational Institute in Tracy.

Now I was taking a 12-month internship at the church after having my parole transferred to Stockton. As an intern, I served as the men's ministry director. During that year Pastor was showed the church who I was and what I could do, then he hired me. I had the office, the title and the influence of the church, but time was about to take its toll. In no time I found that married life was something I was not equipped for.

I was working at the church but I was looking for something that my wife, the church, my title, even my education or influence was not providing. I knew how to be *Pastor French* in public but in just a couple years I was destroying my marriage from internal struggles.

I didn't know it then, but I wanted more. I wanted to see more than church folk, and do more than church stuff. That sounds bad, but church stuff just gets old when you know there's something over the wall. There had to be more. I do believe the western presentation of this *Messianic Message* has been distributed primarily to the benefit of the power structure rather then to disseminate God's love and compassion globally, which happens to be the Alpha and Omega of God's will. The church is rooted in tradition which is definitely needed, but the church is a vessel made up of individuals bearing the message of the Messiah. A message much bigger than those I learned in Sunday school or bible college.

The message is not personal holiness, that's a vague element of it. The message is not bible study, although we learn much from it, it soon becomes repetitive babble without implementation. The message is not church membership or conferences. The message of the messiah is the *maximization* of each life experience, translated into love towards God's creation.

Love is defined in Hebrew as *ahavah*, which is rooted in the Aramaic word *hav* and literally translates as "give." Therefore the eternal message is to *Give* and that's love.

On the surface it appears that I had progressed, but like much of the church, I just cleaned up well. I had a closet filled with new suits and shirts that fit the atmosphere and order of the beautiful sanctuary and ceremonies, but true progression and growth eluded me.

James E. French

Through all of my readings, lessons and teachings, I realized that the great commission is not about doing church, but rather loving people and serving the forgotten and the least of these. The absence of this in the church perplexed me and I was determined to do what I could to serve those who were not being served.

James E. French

CHAPTER SEVEN

Optimistic Gratitude

God's will is not an itinerary but an attitude.
                    ~Andrew Dhuse

No Bondage
We flew out of America on July 4, 2015. I along with my wife Barbara were headed to the Bahamas where I had the amazing honor of officiating a wedding barefoot in the white sands of beautiful Nassau for two of my closest friends. Mr. & Mrs. Dillard & Cheryl Davis. It was a day of political deliverance that lit the sky coast to coast and it was so apropos as I was celebrating freedom.

While freedom was being realized I was losing my amazing wife. Barbara and I had our fair share of problems. We also had a lot of great times, but it was becoming increasingly evident that I was not prepared.

After six amazing days in the Bahamas it was clear that my marriage was ending. I was still wearing the scars of incarceration like thermal underwear and it was a problem. A problem that I was not equipped to fix at the time. Looking back from the terrace at the white sands, water slides, and luxurious surroundings of the Paradise Island Atlantis Resort, it was quite an upgrade. Such a long way from Folsom Prison. I sat in paradise replaying in my mind the journey of this little boy from San Diego who was abandoned at birth, warded to the court, adopted into blessings, schooled for success, seduced by rebellion, addicted to crime and accepted the consequences.

We flew out of the Bahamas on July 9, 2015. This was significant because it was exactly 15 years to the hour that I was released from prison.

As the city was gearing up for its independence celebration the next day, I couldn't help to think about the irony of the situation. Both of these countries received freedom from the same bondage, British rule.

I know a little something about bondage, incarcerated for 23 years of my life. County jail, rubber rooms and California State prisons from San Diego to the Oregon border had been my places of residence.

I was far from just another gang banging, drug addicted, chain-smoking, violent convict. I was in pursuit of liberty. Liberty that did not exist in the vacuum of illusion, perfect order and harmony, but rather the liberty that exist in the chaos of reality.

Choosing the Message Over the Messenger

While I worked through the chaos to overcome the ghost that chased me and served as a reminder of my past I was growing in popularity. I was teaching, preaching and even delivering keynote messages. I spoke for my undergraduate class at the University of Phoenix where I earned a Bachelor of Human Services degree after my release in 2000.

For ten years, I was employed as a cultural competence instructor at the University of the Pacific in Stockton, California and as the Northern California field director by Prison Fellowship ministries. The ministry was growing and the congregation loved Reverend Frenchie.

We would have two hundred men coming to our conferences and retreats. There were 60 men coming out every other Saturday to the Heroes Fellowship at the church, an open forum teaching and everybody loved it.

I was committed to my position in the church, but felt more conflicted because of my private life and the expectations of what a pastor was supposed to be.

The messenger over the message syndrome, which focused the attention on the person delivering the message, rather than the message itself was losing its grip on me.

I made a decision to leave everything I worked for and resign from my position at the church. Not long after I left the church my marriage hit rock bottom. Barbara was lovely as ever, but I had too many ghost and we both ran out of energy to make our marriage work. We separated, tried counseling and talked it out, but it was too late.

We took down the wedding portrait not long after Barbara and I returned home. It was at the foot of the stairs in the last residence we would ever share with each other. We couldn't bare to walk down those stairs one more time looking at the smiles of a couple who allowed love to slip away.

Like I said, we took down the portrait and the story begins, right where it ends...friends again.

Friendship
We talk about it as though friends are a dime a dozen, but the truth is that there are only ever a few. True friendship is often forged in strenuous circumstances. and that is what I have ultimately discovered. I thought I found my true love, but I

certainly found my friend and that is where it ends right here where it began ... we're still more than.

-Friends.

It's complicated it's emotional and quite nice when the friendship outlast romance.
... and so it ends where it began.

Friends again ... Thank you Barbara Diane

James E. French

CHAPTER EIGHT

Our Gang

No God, no peace. Know God, know peace.
~Author Unknown

Set Trippin'

My story is a dime a dozen, but what I got from it definitely is not. Your particular story makes the difference. The lessons, the experiences and the wisdom that helped me see over the wall was invaluable. My catalyst for writing this book was to share what I have received from the journey,. The goals is not to influence you, but inform you. Now that I am 58 years old, divorced and starting over, my perspective has evolved.

My hope is that just as I have learned from those that have spoken into my life and shared their journey's, I hope someone will be blessed by my raw truth. Some will be offended, but some will be inspired.

One of the biggest lessons I have learned in 58 years is that you can look right at what you think is love, and be wrong as hell. Unconditional love is a very rare beast and it is camouflaged very well. There is no way to tell until you experience it. There is no way to really know until you get to that unconditional moment and see how much love is left.

The people who are right there with you when you are broke and ashamed are the ones who are there to pick you up, help dust you off, take you to Starbucks, and listen to you moan. Those are the ones that are really there for you.

I have learned that family isn't always blood and commitment in any relationship is an advantageous element.

Embracing Freedom

My freedom is building. It's a freedom to navigate my dreams and plot a new course with purpose. I read somewhere that if you do not start building your own dreams someone will pay you to build theirs. I know I was created to uplift, inspire and motivate.

Over the past 10 years, Angel Tree has partnered with my nonprofit organization, *Only God*

Ministries which has held events for the forgotten all over the Stockton area.

Our toy drive connects us by contributing toys galore to help volunteers deliver gifts for children throughout the central valley every Christmas.

Other organization events include OG on ice (our ice skating outing), annual Easter egg hunt and the OG"Man"camp, all done with amazing volunteers. There is an ancestral destiny rising up in me that wants me to serve, care and help others. I do not want people to hurt because I have been hurt and I have hurt others before.

James E. French

CHAPTER NINE

Only God

Peace is not the absence of affliction, but the presence of God.

~Author Unknown

Maturing in the message
From prison to the pulpit to the public, I have sewn together a tapestry that tells a story of my existence before and after it evolved into purpose. In my quest for the truth, I have been in search for avenues to share hope to the widows, orphans, convicts and the homeless. A message for the forgotten and stepped over that resonates with my life.

I often say, "Christ was born in a manger because the shepherd's couldn't get in the palace, but the Kings could get in the barn."

Christ chose the fishermen who where unbecoming, rather than the Pharisees who were and Abraham's Covenant, but Christ chose his preachers from the dirty finger-nailed fishermen.

Why did He choose these unlikely men? Could it be that Christ was disappointed in the synagogue or organized performance? Maybe He was sick of men trying to rule His people? When the people wanted King Saul, God was there to say, "You don't need a king." The judges were horrible as well as the kings.

He said, "I am your king!"

I believe this message has been lost and many still find themselves in search of a king here on earth.

At the beginning of Luke 15, the Pharisees are talking about Jesus hanging out with the regular folks. The first one says, "Look at Him over there hanging out with those sinners." Jesus must have overheard him because He says to the sinners and the publicans,

Yeah they think they got it all because my daddy gave them the Word, but they don't know how to carry it. I am over here talking to you and they have a problem with it because they don't know who you are, but let me tell you who you are...You are like that one sheep that got lost and the shepherd still had 99, but left to go find the lost sheep. You are like that man who had a son who took the money and left, but when the son came back home he gave him a party to welcome him home.

Jesus called it His lost and found similar to the lost and found in church. Every church has a lost and found box. You can look in the lost and found box and see a pair of glasses, someone's Bible or an earring. What is interesting about that box is if you look inside, there is nothing in there that is important to you. You might pick up the glasses and put them back down because it is someone else's stuff, which has no value to you. Many people are still like the lost objects in that box. They have lost hope, they do not know that love, redemption, protection, mercy and giving still have value.

I want people to look in that box and know they are no longer lost. We need to know that we belong to truth, purpose and light. We must treat others like it. If you looked in that box and saw your friends' glasses you would get them because you value your friend and you know her glasses are important to her. We are supposed to value God yet we step over hurt people every day. We even do it on our way to church to praise God.

The purpose of the church is to identify with the land and infiltrate it with love. Jesus could have pulled the God card at anytime, but He didn't. In contrast, the modern church needs to have a microphone, a big building, a huge congregation, fancy suites, a large band and a mega choir all the time. The question is, are we finding our purpose? Our purpose is to give love and care about more than just ourselves and our comfort zones. This is a lesson I didn't learn in seminary, but on the yards, chapels and cell blocks of state prison.

On this journey I learned that I don't know as much as I thought I knew about God, man life, death, heaven and earth. My favorite Bible story is of the blind man in John 9 who encountered the word of God for real. A Jewish boy raised in the Torah, but when asked to declare his theological opinion on the deity of Christ he simply said I don't know.

He knew what happened to him. He was blind and then he could see. He told them to keep their robes, candles and theological perspectives. He was ready to enjoy his new found vision. This was a manifestation of God's works and thus revealed God himself and his purposes on earth.

When I was in PRISON, I was angry set tripping and confused. When I went from parole to the PULPIT I was still set tripping, but now for the church. Today, In the liberty of PURPOSE, I find a PLACE for peace, purpose and enlightenment!

James E. French

CHAPTER TEN

Original Gospel

I believe in the sun even if it isn't shining. I believe in love even when I am alone. I believe in God even when He is silent.

~Author Unknown

Sermons vs. History

I've started reading again, studying and exploring creation for truth. Daring to ask hard questions bracing myself to accept the answers. Truth and tradition stand nose to nose in the center ring.

There's more to know about Genesis chapter six and The Sumerian Tablets, more to know than the Cannon endorses or Rome's influence will disclose. If you are in search of this enlightenment the book of Enoch is worth a peek, I guarantee it!

There's more to know about the systematic deception and strategic lies regarding history, culture and the origins of Black people in the west. I'm asking real questions now and finding real answers outside of my trained norm. I have discovered that if it does not disturb your norm it isn't causing or effecting change. I believe this message will disturb norms down to the core of those who believe and are in tune to receive the blessings from our Father.

There is much more to unveil and I do not think that I should be trying to raise my right hand too fast to any one interpretation of what this experience from life to death is all about.

I do believe there is virtue in recognizing and honoring the markers and landmarks of our journey. I found my sight in Christ. It was the message of the Messiah that put me on the floor of my cell back in Folsom Prison when I was just 33 years old. I learned and surrendered to love over hate, and peace over war because of an encounter with Christ, and the Bible.

I learned from that message that I wanted and even needed love again despite all the years of false emotion or playing a role. The same stories exist throughout religious discipline, and because of the training I received in this message, there is no doubt that I'm a better man. I have learned not to judge love through religion.

Globally, there are demonstrations daily of the power that floored me and changed my life, and it's not confined to the church, a country or any religion.

Anywhere you go, you know that a standing ovation is a show of honor, and you feel it. You know the feeling you get when you see a rescue at sea, miners trapped underground make it out alive or people digging through the rubble of a disaster, franticly and passionately searching for survivors. You know what you are looking at when you see a mother playing peek a boo with a baby, or a father fishing on a lake with his son. You know what truth, honesty and dignity are no matter what spiritual discipline a person claims.

I stopped judging others when I stopped allowing others to judge me. I was able to learn from every experience. I'm recognizing that love is the key while opening the doors to truth and purpose.

Throughout my journey I have been in search of knowledge. Proverbs 2 has been my reminder that has kept me focused and on course as I continue to expose my self to truth.

My son, if you receive my words
and treasure up my commandments with you,

making your ear attentive to wisdom
and inclining your heart to understanding;

yes, if you call out for insight
and raise your voice for understanding,

if you seek it like silver
and search for it as for hidden treasures,

then you will understand the fear of the Lord
and find the knowledge of God.

James E. French

CHAPTER ELEVEN

Ordinary Genius

Only God can judge me so I'm gone, either love me or leave me alone.

~Sean Carter

Positioned to prosper
Only God can define my journey. This evolving navigation of sunsets and storms has lead me to believe that Only God can lead me.

Only God, as defined in ancient assertions and present day purpose.

Only God as defined by the Equinox, revealed in detail of archeological rocks, passed down in oral tradition and read in what was written.

Only God can give you what it takes not to quit, don't quit!

There are so many things that give us every reason to quit on ourselves, quit on our dreams and destiny, but God is the architect and He desires more of you.

Incarceration, divorce, unemployment, betrayal and the ghosts from our experiences threaten to haunt our tomorrow. When I was unemployed in Stockton, California for three years, I applied for job after job to no avail. The stigma and pressure was horrible. I wanted to work but, I was either too old, an ex-con, not experienced, Black, and the list goes on. Still, I was determined to keep going.

As for me, deep down ...
I just wouldn't stop. I pushed on with pure hustle and heart, but it still was not enough. My world needed to reset. I knew my worth never changed nor did my calling or passion to help others. While my own judgement was trying to drown me, I pushed on — feeding homeless folk and helping ex-offenders get reacquainted with family. Whoever hit my phone in crisis previously, still has 24-hour access today.

I want to encourage someone who might need more than hearing the words *Don't quit.* Maybe you need to know that God has you covered and will carry you when you feel like you don't have strength to continue on your path.

Today my most amazing dreams are lighting every inch of the sky, day and night because I did not give up on myself, and neither has My God. To embrace what my God had prepared for me I had to learn from folks that refused to quit. I didn't quit — no matter what! No matter what *they* say — don't quit on you!

My life is more than religion and status quo. When everything was taken from me, including my freedom and I felt like I had nothing left. That's when I had to remember what kept and sustained me on this journey. What sustained me during my years of incarceration and helped me to keep pushing rather than being squeezed until I could no longer breathe was the fact that I wasn't alone. God was with me.

Only God is my mantra. Only God knows and Only God cares. I can't explain how or why, I just believe that Only God can judge me, protect me, provide for me and lead me to my purpose. Only God can really make sense of such a crazy life.

It's all about purpose!
My life, my adventures, my love, and my loss — it has to have purpose. To be quite honest, Only God knows the whole story. It has been a steady progression of opportunity and favor directly from the hand of God that has brought me from foster care, addiction,

gang life and 23 years in prison. My testimony has become my credentials.

I have shared this story with you to encourage you on the journey to finding your purpose, but also encourage myself. Through your storms and sunsets, loves and losses your best days are still ahead of you.

I've been to the Emerald City, I've seen behind the curtain and I learned that Oz never gave the Tin Man anything that he didn't already have.

I am over the wall and the view is exquisite.

The End

James E. French

I CAN SEE CLEARLY NOW

Orating Greatness

I bought my glasses today.
Lens Crafters had a special.
$99 out the door for a pair of single vision lenses.
Of course, I need progressive no-line bifocals, but that was only $169.
I wound up with the $275 Ray bands with the light tent and silver & Black frames...
Love these glasses by the way.
But it is not about the glasses it is about the lenses.

Lenses are how we see the world.
Sociological lenses, religious lenses, family & traditional lenses...different views, and points of view all seen through.
Those lenses...
If you wear glasses you know what it's like to put on another person's prescription.
Blur... Right?

Blurred is no way to see,

So getting my glasses was somewhat of a milestone on this journey of mine...

Because for too long I have been comfortable with blurred vision, someone else's prescription so to speak.

I contend, that we all see life through the lenses we have been given by our families, our cultures and our tradition. We see things the way we are taught to and we build our expectations around this training. Needless to say we are often instructed in ways that are irrelevant and even destructive to the journey we ultimately travel. From high school trigonometry that you never use, to political and religious positions that often change and evolve. No one's fault just the fact, that I got my glasses today...
I am wearing my prescription and I am seeing clearly.

No more blurred vision in the remainder of this journey.
I have new lenses, in my prescription, offering a prospective a clear perspective of
who I am and what I must do.

www.OGMinistries.org

James E. French

CPSIA information can be obtained
at www.ICGtesting.com
Printed in the USA
LVHW081031111221
705930LV00029B/2405

9 780997 987027